Management and Leadership

What Can MBA Do in My Workday?

First Research Paradigms Applied Edition, March 2019

Artwork (p. 1) by Eric Michael Ayala
Photos (p. 3 - 60) from Pixabay.com
Photo (p. 20): Trojan Horse by A Yakovel 1911
Photo (p. 51) from Flickr by Cliff (no changes made):
www.npg.si.edu/exh/hall2/jadamss.htm
www.npg.si.edu/exhibit/VicePres/flash.html#/jefferson/0/
Copy editing: Academic Copyediting
Design: Research Paradigms Applied, LLC

What Can MBA Do in My Workday?
Edited book collection

Alex Stajković, *Editor in Chief*
Kayla Sergent, *Executive Editor*

This edited collection aims to advance evidence-based
application of the topics typically covered in the MBA programs.

Book 1. Management and Leadership
         by Alex Stajković and Kayla Sergent

LIBRARY OF CONGRESS CONTROL NUMBER: 2019936784

ISBN: 978-1-7338275-0-8

About the Authors

Alex Stajković, Ph.D.
Professor of Organizational
Behavior and M. Keith Weikel
Distinguished Chair
in Leadership, Wisconsin
School of Business,
UW-Madison.
www.stajkovic.biz

Kayla Sergent, Ph.D., CPA
Assistant Professor of
Organizational Behavior,
Edgewood College
www.sergent.biz

Dedication

This book is dedicated to our Executive and Evening MBA students. We have learned from you as much as you may have learned from us. It was fun tossing pearls of wisdom around, debating them, and spending time together in the classroom discussing these topics.

Table of Contents

Introduction   2

Part I: Management and Leadership   7
   Management   8
   Strategic Management   8
   Leadership   12
   Quick Hits   17

Part II: Transactional Management   19
   Context   19
   A Model of Self-Regulation   24
   Goal Setting   26
      STD Goal Attributes   27
      Boundary Conditions   30
      Effectiveness   34
   Contingent Reinforcement   35
   Negative Feedback Loop   37
   Confidence   40
      Self-efficacy   42
      Core Confidence   43
   Quick Hits   45

Part III: Transformational Leadership   47
   Idealized Influence   48
   Inspirational Motivation   49
   Intellectual Stimulation   52
   Individualized Consideration 54
   Intricacies of Positive Feedback Loop   57
   Quick Hits   58

Conclusion   60
References   62
Index   64

Always Together, Forward Forward

EMBA   CLASS OF 2000

Introduction

Who Cares?

We framed this book using feedback from our students. For example, we would hear:

> "We like these topics. Can you put together something easy to read, still research-based, that we can occasionally go back to remind us of the topics and their work application?"

Here it is. We sent drafts of this book to students for feedback. We cannot think of a better introduction than comments from those who lived through these topics and our banter about them.

> "The book was a great summary of the concepts and the most useful takeaways of the semester."

> "I found this to be a great resource that I can reference after the program to help spark topics we discussed in class and ways to approach different work situations."

> "I really enjoyed reading this, and will actually share with my fiancé so she can get some insight into what we have been learning, as she consistently asks but it is hard to find a summary as good as this."

The underlying current of this book is *moving the needle* - transforming disengaged workers to motivated employees, shifting doubt into efficacy, and progressing from managers to leaders.

So What?

Management and Leadership are taught in almost all MBA programs. Many schools require these topics in an opening class. Paraphrasing a renowned physicist, Robert Oppenheimer, **physics would be really hard if particles could talk.**

In the study of management and leadership, we focus on people. People talk, talk back, and come with different preferences, attitudes, and personalities. Some work less, some are more agreeable, some are open-minded, some are happy, and some are grumpy.

Yet, managers and leaders need to motivate all employees. Good luck doing this in a factually-informed way without some training on these topics.

What power-holders do is often at odds with the best evidence. This is called the doing-knowing gap.

MIND THE GAP

Learning how to motivate and lead employees is fundamental to an organization's success. Half-truths *de jour* are dangerous because they can be partly right. However, these myths are misleading often enough to get many organizations into serious trouble.

How Was Content of the Book Selected?

This book relies on classic theories that have been empirically supported. Why? Evidence-based answers can be applied with a dose of certainty.

We do not present a flavor of the month fad. Motivational speakers and folk psychologists ought not be taken seriously, even if they are entertaining. Making business choices based on fiery proclamations, flimsy data, and equivocal recommendations will lead to questionable results.

Instead, our goal in writing this book is to present management and leadership topics in a useful manner while drawing on foundational empirical research.

Know Before You Go

Nothing in this book is meant to suggest that other areas of business are less important than management and leadership. Tolstoy opens up his novel Anna Karenina with this unforgettable line:

"Happy families are all alike; every unhappy family is unhappy in its own way."

As in families, organizations must assemble the right mix of ingredients to produce a recipe for success. Misery is more idiosyncratic, but few things bring an organization down faster than a demotivated workforce antagonized by insolent leadership and ineffective management.

Developing leadership savoir-faire is a topic Business Schools should increasingly embrace.

What can we do? In our conversations with leaders, a common theme emerges. Many did not have an opportunity to study the psychology of leadership before they found themselves consumed by its demands. They recollect how it was only after their leadership tenure ended that they found time to study the subject that had filled their lives for decades. This book fills this gap by providing an introduction to concepts in the study of management and leadership.

If you enjoy webinars, Alex also has a free 45 minute webinar on Transformational Leadership available at: http://www.stajkovic.biz/media/webinars

Manage processes

Lead people

Part I: Management and Leadership

Is management different from leadership?

Yes, management and leadership entail different activities. But, not for the reasons most assume. Leaders are not mythical, and managers are not simple folk merely trying to keep order on this Earth.

Management and leadership activities are necessary and complementary. Managers are irreplaceable for efficient operations. This focus, though, might inhibit their capacity to inspire above and beyond motivation.

The general differences between management and leadership activities can be summarized as follows:

Manage processes. Lead people.

By focusing on people, leaders inspire above and beyond motivation. Have you ever heard anyone say ...

Let's manage soldiers into battle?

Manager	Leader
John Adams	Benjamin Franklin
Alexander Hamilton	Thomas Jefferson
Pope Bendict XVI	Pope John Paul II
Sam Walton	Richard Branson
Mitt Romney	Barack Obama

Management

Focuses on work processes.

Organizations need management. Lack of specific processes, enforced diligently, translates into doomsday scenarios for businesses. Without management, companies lose order and consistency, eventually undermining a firm's purpose and existence. Data in organizational literature bears out that most businesses cannot function properly and survive in the marketplace without effective management.

Could a messy construction site evolve into a highly functional, esthetic modern building without specific processes that are enforced daily by diligent managers?

Strategic Management

Strategic management, i.e., strategy, strategic planning, boils down to this key question:

What's our

Strategic management covers managerial activities at the macro level of an organization. For example, strategic decisions are often made at the levels of departments, divisions, or organizations as a whole.

Strategic managers decide how to deploy resources and when to obtain new resources to create a competitive advantage. Consider a construction firm bidding for a

Planning
Organizing
Controlling
Evaluating

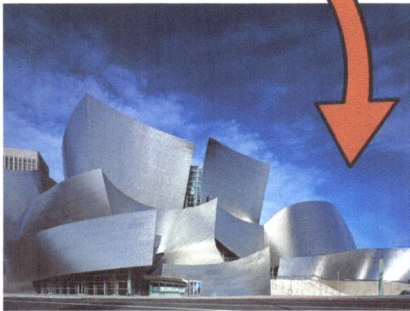

Strategy buzzwords
Value proposition
Asset allocation
Leverage resources
Differentiation
Five Forces
Inimitable
Invest-Divest

You cannot be strategic without strategy.

formula for success?

large contract. Someone at the firm level is thinking about what product mix to offer, at what price, is there existing technology or should we acquire it, can we control cost, do we need a strategic alliance, and what are other market differentiations we can offer?

These are the types of questions that an MBA course in strategy would likely address.

Ready to have some strategic fun?

Strategy is undoubtedly important. Sometimes, though, the rhetoric leverages the lingo beyond what people can take-in with a straight face. For example, think of any three-digit number. Then, select the corresponding buzzword from each of the three lists. Get it? Any combination works! Consider this at your next meeting, neighborhood party, or work it into a conversation at the gym, bar, latte shop - you name it.

List 1
0. total
1. integrated
2. functional
3. systematized
4. sustainable
5. nonobligatory
6. synchronized
7. congruous
8. responsive
9 balanced

691
synchronized
reciprocal
capability

List 2
0. competitive
1. management
2. progressive
3. digital
4. incremental
5. new-generation
6. organizational
7. interim
8. incremental
9. reciprocal

List 3
0. flexibility
1. capability
2. alternative
3. hardware
4. contingency
5. advantage
6. mobility
7. design
8. programming
9. projection

879
responsive
interim
projection

450
sustainable
new-generation
flexibility

168
integrated
organizational
programming

034
total
digital
contingency

715
congruous
management
advantage

And, our all-time favorite
that no list can capture:

Strategic Strategy

Leadership

Focuses on people.

The goal is to inspire above and beyond motivation. The word *motivation* comes from the Latin *movere*, meaning to move. The definition we prefer is ...

> Motivation governs choices among alternative forms of voluntary activity.[1]

Employees are free to pursue numerous activities. Motivation determines which activities they choose. Little happens unless people are motivated. Motivation also governs direction and intensity of behavior. People come to work with a range of motivation. They can be motivated to perform just above the minimum or to go above and beyond.

Low motivation can lead to disengagement. A 2017 Gallup Global survey showed that 67% of employees were not engaged. [2]

This survey also found that 18% of workers worldwide were actively disengaged. These people were purposefully and effortfully engaged in being disengaged from work.

There is untapped potential out there. The question becomes, how can managers tap into that potential?

If people believe they are **tapped-out**, with no motivation left in the tank, then there is nowhere else to turn but to genetics, personality, and pedigrees to explain and improve work performance.

Managers are not trained to inspire above and beyond motivation, but leaders are able to reach these motivation, effort, and performance heights.

Compare and Contrast Exercise

For what it is worth, we see the Old Testament as more of an example of management, and the New Testament as more of an example of leadership.

To complicate this example, would you consider Moses and Joshua to be managers or leaders? In our view, Moses was more of a leader, and Joshua was more of a manager. Do you agree or disagree? Why?

Would you agree with this line of reasoning, respectively, for St. Peter and St. Paul?

Hi. I am attracted to you and would like to acquire, use, and dispose of you when you are no longer useful to me. *Please come be my human capital?*

The primary focus of leadership is on motivating human capital. Like financial capital, humans bring value to an organization.

Although intuitive, not everyone likes the phrase human capital. Some suggest that it equates humans with assets. There is little wrong with being an asset, except that they are typically bought, used, and eventually discarded (e.g., machines).

Consider a famous fable from Antiquity, Aesop's story of the Golden Egg. An "ancient economist" realized that his goose lays golden eggs. He figured he would kill the goose and get all the golden eggs at once (e.g., quarterly profits), versus nurturing it and getting the golden eggs over time (long term perspective). He killed the goose but found no golden eggs.

The moral of the story? Profits come from people. Nurture people and profit will come. Abuse people, and you will get nothing. People first, profits second. Take care of your goose!

Values, Vision, and Mission

Leaders set the values, vision, and mission as the "guardrails" for a path forward. The three concepts coalesce around a core meaning: What philosophical, not only economic, fundamentals do we stand for?

Values are the moral foundations of a company - the basic rights and wrongs. For example, Starbucks believes in providing health care to all employees, not only to those employed full-time.

Vision is a greater good we aim to achieve. For example, Alfred Sloan proposed, "A car for every purse and purpose," to GM shareholders in 1924.

Mission is how we achieve the vision. Ingvar Kamprad, the founder of IKEA, fervently adhered to "Relentless pursuit of efficiency."

If powerholders pursue any values, vision, and mission they will attract followers for whom "anything goes." For example, organizations can disguise dog food in baby formula, lower the unit cost, and charge higher margins. None does it for it is a wrong thing to do.

Quick Hits

1. Managers run the ship according to pre-specifications. Leaders motivate employees to go above and beyond. Leaders assume that human capital can bring value to an organization. Values, vision, and mission set the guardrails for what we do.

2. Leaders are able to inspire employees to go above and beyond by increasing their work motivation. Leadership does not require formal authority.

The issue with trying to be a leader, if that is not your forte, is you may promote yourself into incompetence.

3. Look for fit between what you bring to the table and the demands of the job. If you find fit, you will be more productive and happier.

If the job is not a fit, you can still be productive but at a higher cost. It will take more mental and physical energy for you to accomplish the same outcomes as an individual who is a fit for that job. Misfit will cause wear-and-tear on your mental system.

Take-Home Messages

What it takes to run machines is not the same as what it takes to motivate humans

Take care of the goose first

Person-environment fit matters

Part II: Transactional Management

Why the adjective? It provides further nuance in differentiating the activities of managers and leaders.

What managers do is transactional.

They get what is expected and inspected. They enforce due diligence and compliance.

Consider airport ground traffic. Numerous planes are taxiing, taking off, and landing. Lack of strictly enforced procedures would be a complete disaster.

We distinguish between transactional managers, who focus on enforcing compliance to get things done to specs, and transformational leaders, who focus on transforming the hearts and minds of their followers. Transformation of the belief system leads to above and beyond motivation, effort, and work performance.

Context

The need for transactional managers grew after the advent of agriculture, to say nothing of its role in erecting historic marvels such as the Pyramids of Egypt, the Parthenon, or the Pantheon. We focus on the Industrial Revolution onward. Many current organizations concentrate on traditional sources of competitive advantage (described next). The aim of these traditional sources is to . . .

Obtain a sustainable competitive advantage by creating/using distinctive competencies.

These competitive approaches were conceived by strategic managers, but the success of each one depends on transactional managers doing their jobs.

For this reason, transactional managers contribute to a firm's success by making well-grounded recommendations as to how the business should be competing. Next, we cover a few traditional strategies.

> *Strategy:* **Defines the problem or opportunity, the scope of a firm's activities, explains the reasons those activities will improve performance, and identifies the isolating mechanism that allows a firm to out-perform its competition.**

Strategy ≠ Plan

Strategy matters when there is potential conflict - when interests collide and resolution is needed. In contrast, a plan presumes a sequence of events that allow firms to move from one state of affairs to another. The unpredictability of business affairs, due to chance events, opponents, and mistakes, makes the formulation and execution of strategy an important task of transactional managers.

> **In organizations with superior resources, strategy is a matter of sensible execution.**

One purpose of forming an organization was, well, to organize. Therefore, efficiency was paramount.

Efficiency

Efficiency involves making a product or offering a service with the least amount of time, material, and labor. One way to manage efficiency is to focus on having a **better supply chain** than competitors. Firms can achieve this through vertical integration or horizontal differentiation. From a people efficiency perspective, Scientific Management of Frederick Taylor was the high-point in the late 19th century.

Economies of Scale

The first cousin of efficiency is scale. Economies of scale have consolidated many industries through mergers and acquisitions since the mid 20th century.

As sources of a competitive advantage, efficiency and economies of scale are mostly about competing to...

...Lower Unit Cost

There are many approaches to lowering unit cost. A few examples and terms are provided below.

Variable cost: Changes proportionally with the change in number of units produced. If, for example, the raw materials to make a stool cost $2.50, we would incur this cost for every stool made.

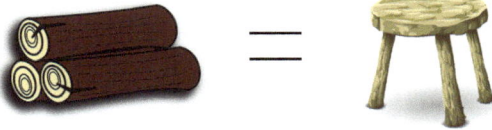

Fixed cost: Capacity related costs that do not vary in the short run (e.g., rent, depreciation, salaries). The more units we produce, the more we can spread-out total fixed costs among the units. This lowers *per unit fixed cost.*

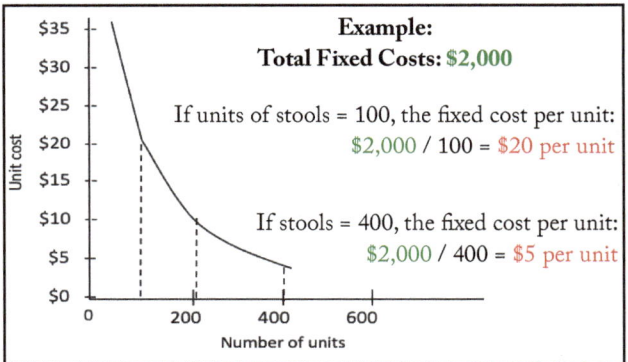

Example:
Total Fixed Costs: $2,000

If units of stools = 100, the fixed cost per unit: $2,000 / 100 = $20 per unit

If stools = 400, the fixed cost per unit: $2,000 / 400 = $5 per unit

Marginal cost: The cost of producing one more unit.

Opportunity cost: The cost of benefits forgone by making one decision over another.

Quality In the 1980s, Edward Deming pushed quality as a new focus in competitive business battles. This quality push manifested itself in two ways.

One is selling products at the same price, but at a higher quality that sells in greater volume. For example, products certified by six sigma quality control are more likely to be sold. The other method is to produce high-quality, luxury items that command a price premium. For example, for every Southwest Airlines that earns margins via cost austerity, there is an Emirates Air that competes on luxury.

The economic benefits of efficiency, scale, and quality are hardly deniable on paper. In practice, their success depends on effective transactional managers.

Other ways to compete include planting the flag, whale watching, price dumping, globalizing, digitizing, mobilizing, branding, opportunity recognizing, differentiating, intellectualizing, and, of course, specializing.

A Model of Self-Regulation

We depict the workings of transactional management through the conceptual framework of self-regulation.

The focus of this model is on closing the negative feedback loop. This approach is empirically supported.

We use a simplified and modified conceptualization of what has been called control theory to depict self-regulation at work spurred by transactional managers.

The components in this model include the following:

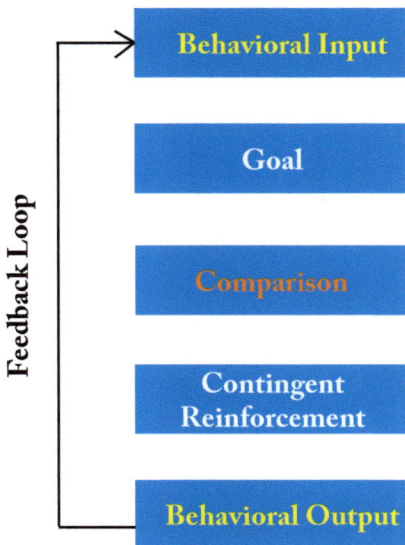

Behavioral Input: As employees strive toward achieving a goal, they provide cognitive and behavioral input toward the pre-set goal.

Goal: The desired performance outcome.

Comparison: At the end of the time period, the performance outcome is compared to the goal, and the difference is evaluated. If performance is below the goal, a negative feedback loop is created.

Contingent Reinforcement: A reinforcer is used to address the feedback loop.

Behavioral Output: A negative feedback loop is closed by a subsequent behavioral output function. Negative reinforcement (either "this or else") is applied to help close the loop.

Think of a thermostat. The temperature is preset to a desired value. When the room temperature is different from the preset value, the device kicks-in to close the gap. This is a rigid portrayal of self-regulation, but in the business world goals must be reached or the process does not operate as intended. If a negative loop is not closed, then negative consequences will ensue.

Discrepancy reduction by closing a negative feedback loop is the hallmark of self-regulation by transactional management. People, but not organizations, have a subconscious tendency to repeat the miseries of their past (repetition compulsion, per Freud). If companies repeat failures, they will go out of business in a hurry.

Apropos, another guiding principle in closing a negative feedback loop at work is for cognitive and behavioral resources to be allocated according to the

principle of least necessary effort.

This principle holds that for self-regulation to be adaptive, people should not allocate less nor more resources to a pre-calibrated goal level than that which is needed. Hence, the process of self-regulation must start with appropriate goal setting.

Goal Setting

Input – **Goal** – Comparison – Contingent Reinforcement – Output

A goal is a defined and valued end. Employees strive to approach desired ends and avoid undesired ends.

Without goals, behavior is aimless. There is nowhere to go, nothing to do, and no standard for comparison.

Goal setting is so "… fundamental to the Western way of thinking, that the circumvention of…" setting a goal and then taking action is "… considered a violation of the rational ideal" [3]

STD goal attributes [4]

Specific

Time-bound

Difficult

Specific. A goal must be specific. Vague goals lack direction. They spread mental resources too thin.

When we conduct executive education seminars on goal setting, we ask leaders to identify critical behaviors. Then, we develop a list that supervisors use to keep track when employees exhibit those behaviors.

To determine if your goal is specific enough, ask yourself this question:

"Can someone unfamiliar with my situation decide if I achieved the goal or not?"

For example, if you set a professional goal to "build my network," what will indicate goal attainment after one month of progress? Use your answer to pre-set the goal. That is, if 10 new connections on LinkedIn in one month indicates attainment, set the goal of 10.

Time-bound. Goals need to be time-bound. Absurdly short deadlines increase difficulty beyond the intended level. In contrast, excessive time lines are not motivating. Imagine setting a goal to earn your MBA in 20 years. How motivating would this goal be today?

When people set a goal too distant in the future, they discount the expected future benefits of goal attainment. When faced with a decision between acting on a short-term or long-term goal, people will choose the short-term goal. For this reason, long-term goals need short-term sub-goals to sustain effort.

Without time-bounds, behavior may not occur. Consider the following example. In the first year of his retirement from politics, Thomas Jefferson did not write many letters to anyone, despite being known for writing letters.

Jefferson apologized to James Monroe and blamed the long silence on "that sort of procrastination which so often takes place when no circumstance fixes a business to a particular time." [5]

Use sub-goals to break-up long-term goals into several short-term goals. Think of sub-goals as bread crumbs that keep you on the right path toward accomplishing your overall goal.

Difficult. A goal needs to be difficult, yet achievable. Easy goals hardly get the competitive juices flowing. If you assign an easy goal, people will stop exerting effort when the easy goal has been reached. Similarly, setting a goal to "do your best" has no effect on performance because "do best" goals have idiosyncratic meanings.[6]

> **Difficult goals direct attention, intensify effort, and help sustain persistence, especially in the face of obstacles.**

What is a difficult goal? A rule of thumb is to set the goal at the . . .

. . . 90th percentile of performance.

For instance, if the top 10% of employees are assembling products at a defect rate of 2%, then the manager should set the goal at 2% for all employees. This assumes all employees are capable of performing at a 2% defect rate. Goal setting is a motivational technique. It assumes the other 90% of employees are not performing at this level because of insufficient motivation – not lack of ability or skill.

> **Given ability and knowledge, there is a positive linear relationship between goal difficulty and performance.**

Boundary Conditions

Moderate the effectiveness of goals on performance.

Confidence. Even cherished goals will be forsaken if employees doubt they can do what it takes to attain them. Doubt is one reason people behave sub-optimal in a goal pursuit even when they know what to do.

> "If you believe you achieve, if you doubt you go without." [7]

Acceptance and commitment. Employees do not pursue a goal just because they can. They pursue goals that they accept and are committed to reaching. This is also known as psychological attachment.

No goal commitment, no goal pursuit.

The need for goal commitment is amplified for . . .
- Assigned goals because buy-in from employees is not always immediate.
- Difficult goals because attaining these goals requires more effort and prolonged endurance. Yet, these goals have a lower probability of success.

The bottom-line is leaders can set any goal they choose for employees. But, if the employees are not committed to those goals or they lack confidence in their ability to achieve them, then their motivation and subsequent effort will probably be insufficient to reach the goal. In this scenario, theory did not fail; application of goal-setting theory failed.

Feedback. Setting goals without providing feedback is as nonsensical as providing feedback without goals.

Feedback aids performance by clarifying the task; it provides knowledge on prior performance, quantity and quality of outcomes, and it shows ways to improve.

Employees pursuing a goal need feedback. Else, if performance is not on track with the pre-set goal, how will employees know that improvements are needed?

Providing feedback without a goal is a slippery slope. Without a goal, employees are vulnerable to having targets arbitrarily moved mid-stream by their bosses.

Feedback should be set with a PIGS model:

Positive in the manner of delivery. This is not fabricating facts to sound positive.

Immediate follows the principle of reinforcement theory. The closer feedback is in time to performance, the more likely it is that employees will connect it with related behaviors.

Graphic feedback provides for easy visual comparisons of performance outcomes to a goal.

Specific instead of vague generalizations.

Effectiveness

Goal setting has been supported in about a thousand studies. A survey of business professors rated goal setting first in both scientific rigor and practical importance out of 73 theories of organizations.[5]

Goals are not without side-effects

1 Difficult goals attached to lucrative reinforcement, lax oversight, and a culture that makes it easy to rationalize shady practices, can lead to unethical decisions and cutting corners to reach the goal.

2 Goals increase focus, but too much focus can create tunnel vision. This causes employees to miss other important factors in the periphery of the goal. In a study with 24 radiologists, researchers inserted a gorilla 48 times larger than the average nodule, and 83% of radiologists did not register the gorilla! Eye tracking software proved they saw it, but tunnel vision precluded recognition of it. [9]

3 Behavior guided by goals is, by definition, goal-dependent. Consider taxi drivers. On rainy days, there is greater opportunity to earn more money. Yet, there are less taxi drivers on rainy days. Why? Because when drivers reach their goal earlier in the day, they simply go home sooner.

If you are not sure what your career goals are, write your own obituary. What would you like people to say about your work achievements? Use that as a goal and work backwards in connecting it to action.

Contingent Reinforcement

Employees face goals that compete for mental resources, physical energy, and time. Their choice of which goal to pursue is often influenced by the contingent reinforcement attached to goal options.

> "The effect of contingently applied positive reinforcement on behavior is one of the most agreed-upon findings in organizational literature." [10]

To increase desired behaviors, managers can use positive reinforcement or negative reinforcement.

Positive reinforcement is application of a desired reinforcer immediately following a desired behavior.

Three positive reinforcers in organizations include:

Money

Social Recognition

Feedback

Negative reinforcement involves threatening to enact a punishment if behavior fails to meet a goal. For example, consider a manager who threatens to take away an employee's company car if the goal is not met. The aim of the threat, or negative reinforcement, is to encourage the employee to meet the goal.

To decrease undesired behavior, managers can use extinction or punishment.

Extinction is ignoring the undesired behavior, hoping it will go away overtime if nobody reacts. Behavior after extinction usually spikes first and then declines.

Punishment by application is applying a negative stimulus following an undesired behavior. Punishment by removal is removing an existing positive reinforcer.

Whether an employee is reinforced or not, and whether reinforcement is negative or positive, will depend on the self-regulation feedback loop.

Negative Feedback Loop

Input – Goal – **Comparison** – Contingent
Reinforcement – Output

After the time-bound of goal pursuit has expired, a
manager compares actual performance to the goal.
If this comparison indicates that performance was
below the goal, a negative feedback loop is created.

Negative feedback loops need to be closed.

Input – Goal – Comparison – **Contingent
Reinforcement** – Output

The principle behind reinforcement is that employee
behavior is a function of its contingent consequences.
Employees will guide their behavior by past
experiences. This is called history of reinforcement.

Thorndike's Law of Effect

Behavior followed by a negative consequence will
tend to decrease in frequency.

In light of a negative feedback loop, the manager
wants any ineffective behaviors to stop. Consequently,
a transactional manager is likely to apply some form
of negative reinforcement. Negative reinforcement
means "either this or else," where *this* means achieve
the goal and *else* is nothing good.

Paradoxically, negative reinforcement is meant to have positive effect on goal-directed behavior by increasing desired behavior, but its mechanics are typically viewed as threatening.

> **Negative reinforcement is essentially an ultimatum for the future; but, there is still a shot an employee can avoid it by reaching the goal.**

An example of progressive negative reinforcement, though not in a work context, is the ten plagues of Egypt, as described in the book of Exodus in the Old Testament of the Bible.

In short, Moses informs Pharaoh what he must do. Moses warns that if Pharaoh refuses to let the people go, then bad things will happen. Pharaoh refuses each time, and each time his refusal is followed by a plague.

Technically or psychologically speaking, the negative reinforcement used by Moses on Pharaoh was ineffective either because the Pharaoh mis-perceived the severity of the consequences, did not care about the potential negative outcomes, or did not believe the consequences would come to fruition.

Confidence

Input – Goal – Comparison – Contingent
Reinforcement – **Output**

Behavioral output should close the feedback loop.

At this point, employees are aware of how they performed relative to the goal, and they understand what needs to be done to close the feedback loop.

They should be all set to succeed, correct?

Not quite yet.

"... for he who doubts is like the wave of the sea that is driven and tossed by the wind."
(James 1:6)

What if the employee doubts s/he can do what is needed? The employee has the skill and will to close the feedback loop, but simply does not believe s/he can do what it takes to succeed.

Employees haunted by doubt have little incentive to act. They initiate insufficient effort or settle for mediocre solutions. Doubtful employees often think to themselves, "Why even bother trying when I do not believe I can do it?"

> **Confidence is a transformative contributor to adaptive self-regulation by goals, feedback, and reinforcement.**

Self-Efficacy

Self-efficacy is a task and context specific belief.

Self-efficacy for performing a specific task does not necessarily translate to self-efficacy for management.

Self-efficacy is a malleable belief. As such, this belief can be developed. Antecedents to self-efficacy include:

Enacted Mastery: Practice with the task.
Vicarious Learning: Observational learning.
Verbal Persuasion: Encouragement from others.
Physiological Arousal: A healthy mind and body.

Thousands of studies have shown a positive relationship between self-efficacy and various work outcomes across methodologies and settings.[11]

Some drawbacks, though, to self-efficacy include:

If self-efficacy can be developed, can it easily be ruined?

Self-efficacy is defined as a narrow variable; thus, it may not capture complexities of job performance.

Can high self-efficacy lead to complacency over time?

Core Confidence

Core confidence differs from self-efficacy. It is a higher-order construct that underlies four observable variables: efficacy, hope, resilience, and optimism.[12]

Trait core confidence cannot be easily developed. On the flip side, though, it cannot be easily destroyed.

> **Trait core confidence is generalizable to a domain of activities. It is not limited to a specific task.**

Trait core confidence has been shown to affect job performance, job satisfaction, and life satisfaction. It has further been shown to mitigate stress, anxiety, and depression of aspiring entrepreneurs. [13]

"Therefore, do not throw away your confidence, which has a great reward."

(Hebrews 10:35)

Quick Hits

1. In self-regulation, input represents behavioral striving toward a goal.

2. Goals are the key part in the self-regulation model. They provide a comparison point for performance outcomes.

3. If a performance outcome is below the goal, a negative feedback loop is created. A negative feedback loop can be closed with negative reinforcement.

4. If employees harbor doubt in their ability to close the feedback loop, even skill and motivation will not be sufficient to enable them to close the loop.

5. Self-efficacy is a "can-do" belief for a specific task.

6. Core confidence emphasizes finding fit between domains you are confident for and the job demands.

Take Home Messages

Set a specific, time-bound, and difficult goal

Compare performance outcomes to the goal

Close the negative feedback loop

Person-environment fit matters

Part III: Transformational Leadership

Since the Industrial Revolution, quality of business education has improved, access to knowledge is more widespread, and sharing of information is profuse. As a result, good management is less of a critical source of competitive advantage. Good managers are easier to find and they come at a lower price than ever before.

If anything, today's organizations have relied so much on managers that, as evidence shows, **most organizations are over-managed and under-led**. This situation leads to under utilization of human resource potential in the workplace.

Coupled with a drastically changing workplace environment, this thread of events has increased calls for leadership to permeate the conversations on obtaining a competitive advantage. Wrenching changes confront today's organizations. Greater job demands require greater levels of work motivation.

> **Transformational leadership focuses on discrepancy creation. Transformational leaders motivate employees to go above and beyond to surpass prior goal levels.**

To be transformational, leaders engage in four sets of behaviors. These behaviors include Idealized Influence, Inspirational Motivation, Intellectual Stimulation, and Individualized Consideration. Together, we call these sets of behaviors the four "I"s.[14]

1. Idealized Influence

Leaders influence employees by modeling. Followers want to be like the leader. They like what you do, how you approach problems, how you treat "little people," and how you comport yourself. When this leader walks through the door at work, employees say, "I want to be like him/her."

It helps to be charismatic to have idealized influence.

Charisma – or *gift* in Greek – refers to attributes causing a profound effect on others, anyplace, anytime, across cultures, industries, and race.

2. Inspirational Motivation

Think of two people. One is compelled by reinforcement to transact effort to a pre-set goal. The other is inspired by a vision, whether of a country, a political candidate, or a company. Those who are transacted will likely act different than those who are inspired. Vision can inspire.

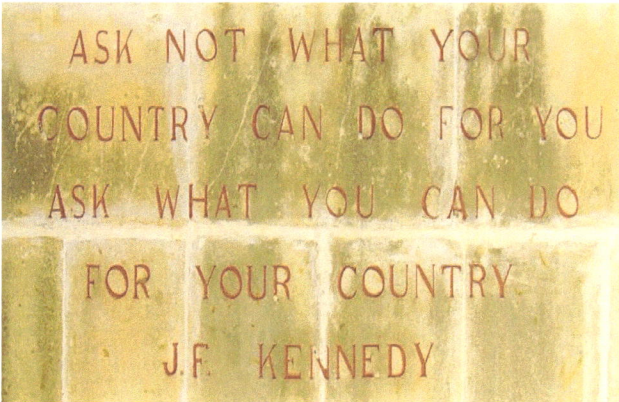

ASK NOT WHAT YOUR COUNTRY CAN DO FOR YOU ASK WHAT YOU CAN DO FOR YOUR COUNTRY.

J.F. KENNEDY

To make people happy.

CRUSH ADIDAS

The following ardent differences in vision, between two close friends, John Adams and Thomas Jefferson, are well documented. The two founding fathers knew each other for 50 years and disagreed almost all of the time on the vision of the American Revolution. Yet, they still tried to explain their visions to each other.

Adams would readily admit that he admired Jefferson, professionally and as a person. But, Adams also disagreed profoundly with Jefferson's political vision of the American Revolution and thought it rested on:

"A seductive set of attractive illusions."

Jefferson's response after his Presidential Inauguration:

"I shall take no other revenge, than … to sink federalism into an abyss from which there shall be no resurrection of it."

After they retired from politics, Adams wrote to Jefferson, "You and I ought not to die before we explain ourselves to each other." [5]

They died the same year, on the same day - July 4th. The last letter each wrote was to the other. Clearly, we can have disagreements on vision without being disagreeable.

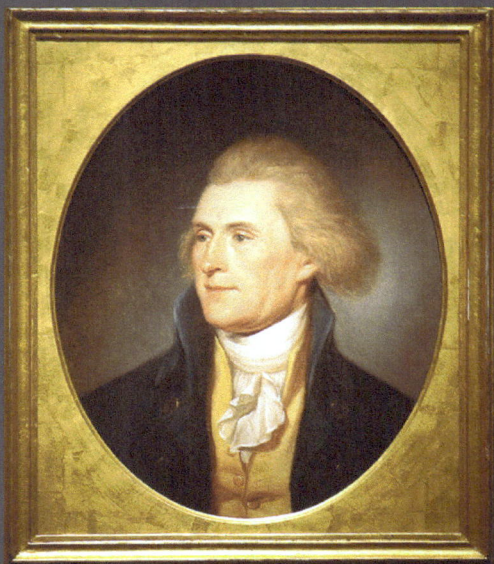

3. Intellectual Stimulation

A leader stimulates followers to be creative and challenges their preconceptions.

Intellectual Stimulation predominantly comes down to creativity. Can a leader stimulate creativity at work to help us gain a competitive advantage in the marketplace?

The source of creativity is debatable – born, made, or primed by the environment? Regardless of your view, creativity is linked to connecting the dots in new ways.

An open question is whether a leader needs to be creative or just be able to spark creativity in others?

Creativity Exercises To Try . . .

1. Brainstorm as many uses as possible for a common object (e.g., brick, hanger) in 2 minutes.

2. Draw two triangles to intersect exactly three times (but not merely "touch" anywhere).

3. Solve these mind teasers . . . .

You are standing on a bridge looking down at a boat full of people. Yet, there is not a single person on board. How can this be?

What five-letter word does every MBA graduate pronounce wrong?

What is one thing that old, wise men and women, regardless of their religion and politics, agree is between Heaven and Earth?

What word from List B can fit in List A?
A. Front, Ski, Melon, Fall
B. Road, Tire, Tower, Cliff

FOUL _____ GROUND

4. Individualized Consideration

How are you going to lead people if you do not truly know them? Maybe your employees are better suited to lead themselves than follow you?

Does the leader know their names?

Does s/he know what they do?

Does/he know their mores, needs, preferences, desires, and fears?

If the answer is no, is it not ostentatious to claim to be a leader of your people? Maybe a "leader" of buildings, machines, and accounts - but not people.

Getting to know your people and your community has always been considered to be good. Why?

Because the more you know someone, the more they

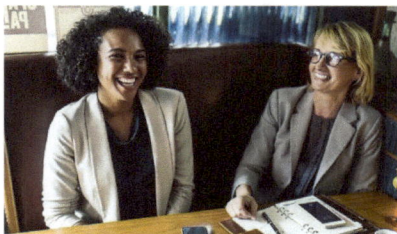

will share. The more they share, the more you can help them to realize their full potential.

This ancient principle has been complicated in organizations by concerns about harassment. The benefits of social bonding are not in question, but its organizational implementation to everyone's satisfaction is a complex and often sensitive matter.

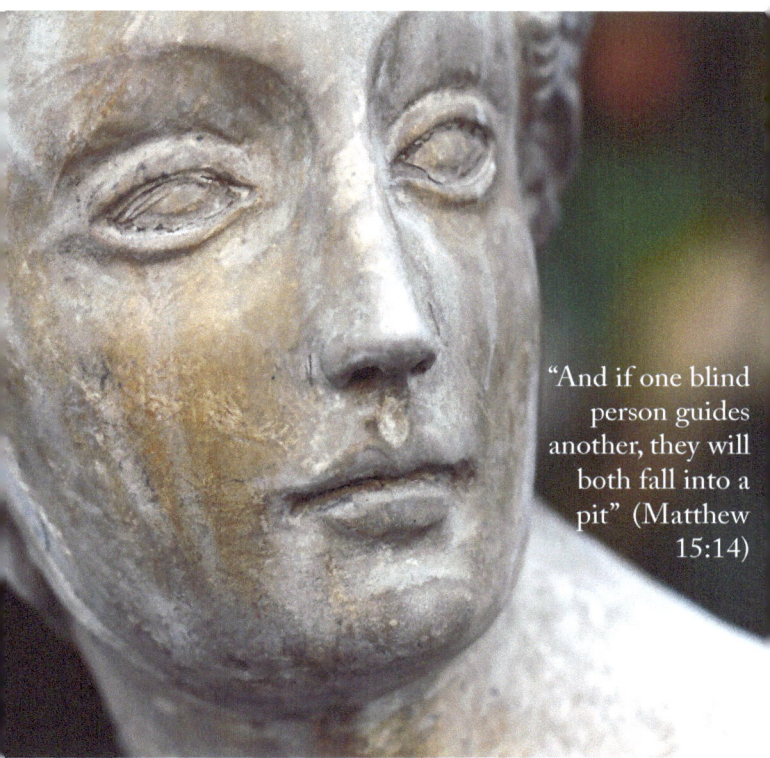

"And if one blind person guides another, they will both fall into a pit" (Matthew 15:14)

Individualized consideration is a desire of the leader to help employees self-actualize. This is the ultimate level of need satisfaction - defined by clinical psychologist, Abraham Maslow.

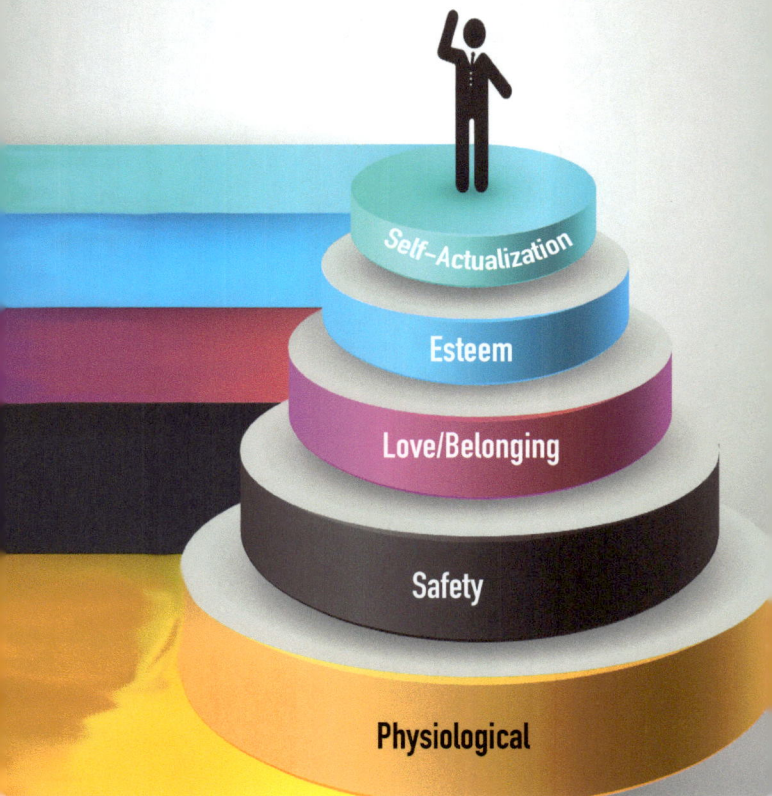

The idea of self-actualization is classic, but it remains unclear how to apply it at work.

According to Maslow, people have to satisfy the lower level needs before moving up to the next level.

Employees are unlikely to share out of the blue their concerns about personal safety and security, let alone their love and belonging needs.

Intricacies of Positive Feedback Loop

A positive feedback loop is intricate for its source can be unclear. It could be that an employee was indeed inspired by transformational leadership and did great.

It could be that the goal was set too low to start with.

As a manager, we do not want employees to close a positive feedback loop by lowering their effort. By the same token, we do not want to leave positive feedback loops open. Demonstrably, the employee can do more.

The most sensible alternative is setting a more difficult goal. But, if we set a higher goal without attaching appealing positive reinforcement, we are basically punishing great work by asking employees to give us more effort for nothing in return.

Setting a higher goal to close positive feedback loops requires accordant levels of positive reinforcement.

Otherwise, employees may feel punished for working hard. A cynical manager may tell workers how pursuing a higher goal is motivating per se. In that case, we recommend the manager be told this next time s/he performs great, since s/he is a true believer in the motivating power of a goal without reinforcement.

Quick Hits

1. Going above and beyond, turning and burning, slicing and dicing, are idioms for doing more with less. Both scholars and practicing managers are on the lookout for motivation techniques and leadership styles that help them achieve this goal.

The advent of transformational leadership has provided empirical evidence that supports positive effects of the four "I"s on motivation and performance.

2. Two of the four "I"s are disposition-like. It is unclear how much they can be changed. For instance, to what extent can charisma be improved in a non-charismatic person through an organizational training?

Would trained charisma come off naturally? Would others in the company buy into it?

The same logic applies to creativity. Where creativity comes from is debated in the literature. But, can a leader become creative through trainings at work?

3. Let us not throw out the baby with the bath water.

If leaders do not embody all four "I"s, they can still use what they have as effectively as possible. There is little that precludes leaders to think about an inspiring vision and ways to get to know their employees better.

Progressing from transactional management to transformational leadership will not occur overnight.

But, one thing is for sure – if you give up trying to make progress, you will never find yourself among transformational leaders.

Long-term leadership effectiveness comes down to moving the needle one day at a time. The race for leadership effectiveness is a marathon, not a sprint. After the Battle of Marathon, the soldier ran 26 miles nonstop to Athens to proclaim one word: Nike! Or, victory! As you decide whether to join the leadership ranks, bear this ancient story in mind.

Conclusion

It is worth reiterating that neither businesses nor leaders can survive without the help of managers.

We conclude with the following story illustrating one of the first examples documented in writing of leaders needing managers:

"The next day ... people sat around Moses from morning till evening. When Moses' father-in law saw all that he was doing for the people, he said, "What is this you are doing for the people? Why do you sit alone, and all the people sit around you from morning till evening?"

And Moses said ... "Because people come to me ... when they have a dispute ... and I decide between one person or another ..."

Moses' father in law said to him, "What you are doing is not good. You ... will certainly wear yourself out, for the thing is too heavy for you. You are not able to do it alone. I will give you advice ... look for able men from all the people ... who are trustworthy and hate a bribe, and place such men over the people as chiefs of thousands, of hundreds, of fifties, and of tens. And let them judge the people at all times. Every great matter they shall bring to you, but a small matter they shall decide themselves. So it will be easier for you, and they will bear the burden with you ... you will be able to endure ..." (Exodus 18: 14-23)

Moses was still having the same headaches. He proclaimed, "I am not able to carry all this people alone; the burden is too heavy for me."

God got involved to help Moses share the burden of leadership. God said, "Gather for me seventy men of the elders of Israel … and they shall bear the burden of the people with you, so that you may not bear it yourself alone." (Numbers 11: 14-17)

What to Know Before You Go

Manage processes, lead people

Person-environment fit matters

Set specific, time-bound, and difficult goals

Provide PIGS feedback

Close feedback loops

Believe to achieve

To be a transformational leader, try:

Idealized Influence
Intellectual Stimulation
Inspirational Motivation
Individualized Consideration

Focus on finding fit

References

1. Vroom, V. (1964). *Work and Motivation.* San Francisco, CA: Jossey-Bass Publishers Classics

2. Gallup. (2017). *State of the Global Workplace.* Washington, DC: Gallup Press.

3. Bourgeois, L. J., III. (1980). Performance and consensus. *Strategic Management Journal,* 1, 227-248.

4. Stajkovic, A.D., & Sergent, K. (2019). *Cognitive Automation and Organizational Psychology: Priming Goals as a New Source of Competitive Advantage.* New York, NY: Routledge.

5. Ellis, J. J. (1998). *American Sphinx: The Character of Thomas Jefferson.* New York, NY: Vintage Books.

6. Locke, E. A., & Latham, G. P. (2013). *New Development in Goal Setting and Task Performance.* New York, NY: Taylor & Francis.

7. Stajkovic, A. D. (2016) Alex Confidence and Performance Talk. *Webinar* available at https://www.youtube.com/watch?v=cXoR3gDn-18

8. Miner, J. (2003). The rated importance, scientific validity, and practical usefulness of organizational behavior theories: A quantitative review. *Academy of Management Learning & Education,* 3, 250-268.

9. Drew, T., Võ, M. L. H., & Wolfe, J. M. (2013). The invisible gorilla strikes again: Sustained inattentional

blindness in expert observers. *Psychological Science*, 24, 1848-1853.

10. Stajkovic, A.D., & Luthans, F. (2001). Differential effects of incentive motivators on work performance. *Academy of Management Journal*, 44, 580-590.

11. Stajkovic, A.D., & Luthans, F. (1998). Self-efficacy and work-related performance: A meta-analysis. *Psychological Bulletin*, 124, 240-261.

12. Stajkovic, A. D. (2006). Development of a core confidence-higher order construct. *Journal of Applied Psychology*, 91, 1208-1224.

13. Stajkovic, A.D., Lee, D., Greenwald, J. M., & Raffiee, J. (2015). The role of core confidence higher-order construct in self-regulation of performance and attitudes: Evidence from four studies. *Organizational Behavior and Human Decision Processes*, 128, 29-48.

See also this short video, *What is Confidence?* Available at https://www.youtube.com/watch?v=HOU0BbHnQgU

14. Bass, B.M., & Riggio, R.E. (2006). *Transformational Leadership.* Mahwah, NJ: Lawrence Erlbaum Associated, Publishers.

Index

Aesop's fable 15

Bible quotes/references 13, 38, 40, 43, 55, 60-61

Confidence 30, 40 - 43, 45

Creativity exercises 53

De-motivation 5, 12

Feedback 2, 33, 61

Goals 26 - 34, 61

Human capital 14 - 15

Idealized influence 48

Individualized consideration 54 - 56, 61

Inspirational motivation 49-51, 61

Intellectual stimulation 52 - 53 , 61

Leadership 3, 7, 12- 16, 47 - 59

Management 3, 7, 8, 19 - 23, 37 - 38

Maslow 55 - 56

Mission 16

Motivation 4, 12

Moving the needle 3, 12

Negative feedback loop 25 – 26, 37 - 38

Person–environment fit 17, 45, 61

Positive feedback loop 57

Quick hits 17, 45, 58

Reinforcement 25 - 38, 57

Self-efficacy 42, 45

Self-regulation 4 - 25

Strategic management 8 – 11

Strategy 20 - 23

Transactional management 18 - 45

Transformational leadership 46- 59

Tunnel vision 34

Values 16

Vision 16, 49 - 50

www.ingramcontent.com/pod-product-compliance
Lightning Source LLC
Chambersburg PA
CBHW041005210326
41597CB00001B/20